ARKANSAS
A PHOTOGRAPHIC CELEBRATION

FOREWORD BY DAVID PRYOR

AMERICAN & WORLD GEOGRAPHIC PUBLISHING

Above: Choose your weapon for a Saturday night dance.
Right: Endless beauty, as seen from Mt. Magazine, Arkansas' highest peak.

Front cover: The White River meanders calmly, looking for the mighty Mississippi. WILLIAM A. BAKE

Title page: The diamond is prominent in the Arkansas flag— this is the nation's only diamond-producing state.
AUDREY GIBSON

Back cover, top left: The lights of the capital city, Little Rock, at night. MATT BRADLEY
Top right: The farmer is the backbone of Arkansas' economy.
MATT BRADLEY
Bottom: There's no more peaceful spot than Lake Chicot in southeast Arkansas. MATT BRADLEY

ISBN 0-938314-97-1

Text © 1991 David Pryor
© 1991 American & World Geographic Publishing, P.O. Box 5630, Helena, MT 59604, (406) 443-2842
Printed in Singapore

ABOUT THE AUTHOR

Senator David Pryor, a native of Camden and lifelong resident of Arkansas, was its governor from 1975 to 1979, and has served his state in the United Stated Senate since then. Throughout his career, he has maintained an interest in historical preservation and natural resource conservation.

Foreword

If I could rest any- where it would be in the heart of Arkansas.

—Davy Crockett, 1834

Like Davy Crockett, I have spent much of my life trying to reach the heart of Arkansas. And as a native and lifelong resident who has traveled its highways and trails, I feel that it should be an easy thing to do.

But it isn't. You start with the land and the crops and the weather, the lakes and mountains, the lowlands and farms, the woods and timber ranges. This is a major beginning, and it takes years of effort, but I don't know that it gets to the heart of things.

It's much easier to find the state's geographic center. Many people believe it has to be in Little Rock, situated at exactly that point where the Arkansas River flows out of the hills and into the flatlands.

Actually, you drive a few miles northwest from Little Rock until you reach what used to be the settlement of Cadron, long ago swept away by time and neglect. All that's left these days is a giant sycamore, some scrub brush, and a sweeping view of the river.

Most folks in the hills believe that, in spite of living in an even row of counties in the north, *they* occupy the heart of the state. It's worth your time to drive that way and see if they're right.

Go north to Conway and then along Highway 65 through Greenbrier, Damascus, and Bee Branch, to Clinton. From there you can fan out to the east into some of the richest farmland anywhere.

Or turn west toward the Ozark National Forest and the most spectacular mountain scenery you can imagine. The term "Ozark" stems from the French, "Aux Ark," meaning "to Arkansas." This derivation is one reason the people in Eureka Springs, for instance, maintain that they live at the heart's core. Old-fashioned Eureka, although pure Arkansas, is one of the nation's unique vacation spots.

A slight turn from Clinton to the northeast will lead to Mountain View and the authentic folk music of the Rackensack fiddles and banjos. "Rackensack," by the way, was an early name for Arkansas, as residents of Stone County are quick to remind you.

TOM COKER

Above: *The Arkansas River flows through Petit Jean State Park.*

Facing page: *Hot Springs' Gulpha Gorge—home to campers from all across the country.* MATT BRADLEY

People in the southern part of the state, like those in the north, also lay claim to its center. If you drive south from Little Rock on Highway 167, you cut down the middle of Arkansas on a long, straight road that takes you through Ico, Sheridan, Cross Roads, and Fordyce.

That's where you either turn east and level out on the flat fields of rice, cotton, and soybeans, or turn west and circle through the piney woods that lead down into Texas. Continue south from Fordyce and you'll pass through the oil fields of Union County and into Louisiana.

It's in this part of Arkansas that you're likely to find a hold-over from the days when we were a French outpost. You run across names like L'Eau Frais Creek and Fourche La Fave River. Smack-over was originally named by the French "Sumac Couvert" because it was a small settlement covered with sumac vines. All we did was turn the word into English.

My point is that any choice you make, in whatever part of the state, leads to a picturesque and different section that offers its own peculiar appeal, in a way its own heart. All are distinctly Arkansas, not quite like any other state in the region.

Arkansas forms a patchwork quilt of every make and kind, combining a portion of those varying cultures that surround it on all sides. We're part old south, part western range, part hillbilly, and part midwestern grain field. From the highlands of the Ozark plateau to the cypress bottoms of the Mississippi plain, we offer a contrast of land regions, climate, wild animals, mineral deposits, rock formations, and species of trees.

I'm always impressed that changes and contradictions in the geography of Arkansas often come as abrupt surprises. Just when you get used to the flat fields of soybeans and cotton in northeastern Arkansas, you run di-

Left: *Dams such as this one at Beaver Lake near Harrison harness Arkansas' water wealth for energy needs.*
Inset: *Contrary to popular belief, you can get there from here.* MATT BRADLEY

Above: A screech owl proudly guards its domain in a wooded area near Lepanto in Northeast Arkansas.

Facing page: The banks of Lake Wedington provide a peaceful getaway near Fayetteville.

rectly into Crowley's Ridge, a high and narrow strip of gravel hills that seem to crop up out of nowhere. It's one of the most unusual natural features in Arkansas, stretching 150 miles south from Cape Girardeau, Missouri, to Helena.

The same quick contrast in terrain occurs in the Grand Prairie, which is bordered by bayous and river lowlands. And Mount Magazine, the highest point in the state, is actually not a part of the mountains that surround it but rises in the middle of the Arkansas Valley.

So I guess we have always had an unusual way of doing business. We inhabit a sprawling and diverse terrain, and we thrive on folklore and legend. According to popular belief, the hoot of an owl means a change in the weather, and the howl of wolves before sunset forecasts rain. A mixture of salt and egg yolk will fix a snake bite.

On a grander scale, it was in Arkansas that the New Madrid earthquake in 1811 supposedly changed the course of the St. Francis River and caused the Mississippi to flow backward. We're also the stuff of tall tales and of people who relish a good story.

With its rich array of inconsistencies, what is the glue that holds Arkansas together? I think it's our tendency to run in packs, to melt into formation when it would be just as easy to split apart. Don't get me wrong—we're also proud of our fierce independence. But a dogged sense of community has somehow never failed us.

What started this gathering in groups was a number of family and neighbor events. The first was the early custom of sitting with the sick. Then came log-raising, when men and women met in an open field to build a new home or a church or school. This led to hog-butcherings and hoedowns.

At one time the most popular excuse for a party was the cemetery clean-up on Decoration Day, when children and parents came together wearing cedar wreathes around their necks. Before the picnic they trimmed the wild grass and cockleburrs from their family burial plots.

Then came the favorite pastime of all—sitting and whittling on the courthouse steps every Saturday morning. You still find this group consciousness

realized in such public gatherings as political rallies, cattle auctions, crafts fairs, and boat shows.

Many of these informal events have become annual occasions. Warren has its pink tomato festival every June, and Gillett sponsors a raccoon supper the first week of January. Grady has a fish fry, Gould a turtle derby, and Marshall a strawberry festival.

The Ozark Frontier Trail Festival and Craft Show has been held in Heber Springs each October for many years. It features a sorghum mill, a water-witching demonstration, a pioneer parade, and a firing of muzzle-loading rifles. Waterwitching, in case you didn't know, is a time-honored means of tracking down underground streams and creeks. You walk along with a forked stick cut from a peach or hazel tree, and when you stand over water the pointed end of the limb bends toward the ground.

Above: Weaving skills are passed from generation to generation.

Facing page: Hot Springs' world-renowned Bathhouse Row.

At one Fourth of July picnic in 1822 there were nearly 30 celebratory toasts offered among those gathered for what was proudly billed as "free ice water." Toast number 13 has a special appeal to any elected official, even 150 years later: "Less style and more economy at the seat of government."

We still want economy in government, but in some ways Arkansas has changed since the days of pioneers and muzzleloading rifles, and when our schoolteachers were paid half in cash and half in pigs. We have cars and television and the other modern conveniences we take for granted. Fewer people live on farm land these days and more in towns and cities.

The makeup of our population has also changed. By the end of this century Arkansas will have seen a 139 percent increase in its number of elderly people, a rise that's second only to Florida. Many of our aging began to come to Hot Springs in the 1930s and 1940s, attracted by the legendary waters that continue to restore the body and the soul.

In time these transplanted Arkansans spread out to other parts of the state and came to live in communities designed especially for them. You find in the mountains relatively new towns like Cherokee Village, Bella Vista, and Hot Springs Village, all among the first retirement and recreation centers in the United States.

We have many new faces and spots to visit, new highways and trails, new ways of doing old business. But we haven't changed in the way we greet our visitors. It's with a combination of friendliness and curiosity: I'm proud to see these outsiders, but what are they like?

Remember that the first legend connected with Arkansas involves a wayward traveler who receives a genuine but cautious welcome from an old farmer passing an afternoon on his porch. When you come down to it, not much of real importance has changed since then.

—*David Pryor*

The Helena bridge connects Arkansas and Mississippi.

One of the last livery stables in the country was located in Camden, where it was still a thriving business in the 1930s. Founded by John T. Chidester, the original stable was a major stop for the stagecoach that ran from Washington, D.C. to Fort Worth.

Above: Cotton may no longer be king, but is still important to the region's economy.
Right: The Ozarks' beauty draws visitors from all over the country.

MATT BRADLEY

Above: *A New England–style barn in the Ozarks.*
Left: *The one-room seat of the Three R's at Rocky Branch.*

Facing page: *Arkansas' handicrafts will sweep you off your feet.*

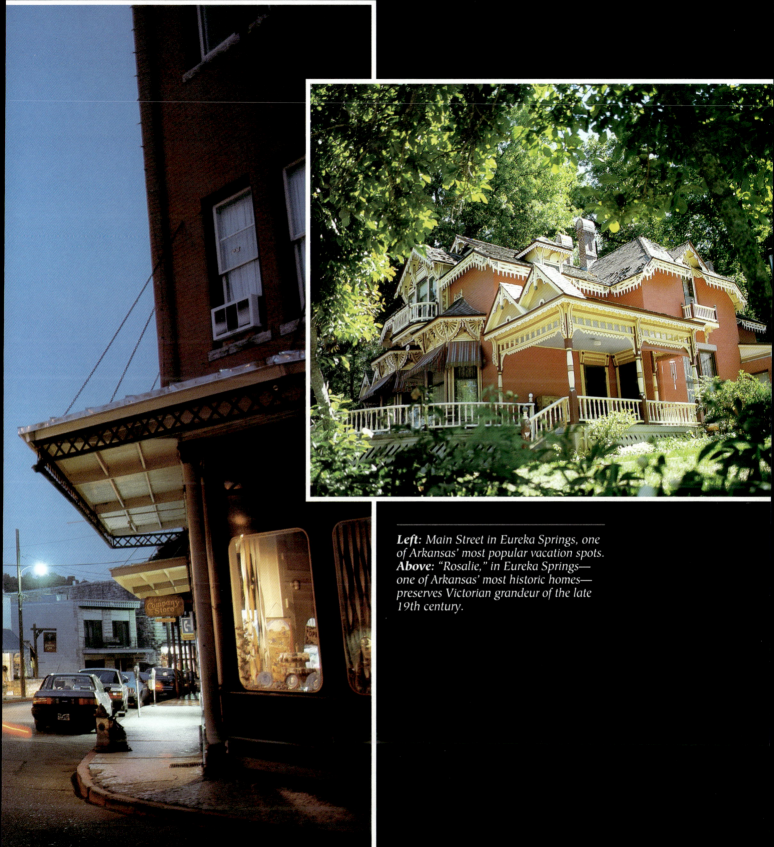

Left: *Main Street in Eureka Springs, one of Arkansas' most popular vacation spots.*
Above: *"Rosalie," in Eureka Springs— one of Arkansas' most historic homes— preserves Victorian grandeur of the late 19th century.*

The New Madrid earthquake hit the northeastern corner of the state in 1811. From dry ground it formed, in one hour, entirely new lakes 20 miles long. A steamboat running from Pittsburgh to New Orleans was caught in the midst of the earthquake and anchored overnight to the edge of an island. The next morning the ship was safe—but the island was gone.

MATT BRADLEY

Above: Cropdusting is a dangerous, but necessary, profession in the Mississippi River Delta.

Facing page: Waterfalls at Devil's Den State Park.

Right: *The Fordyce Bathhouse, restored to its original glory.*
Below: *Stained-glass ceiling artistry inside.*

Facing page: *Azaleas bloom in downtown Hot Springs—Arkansas' premier resort.*

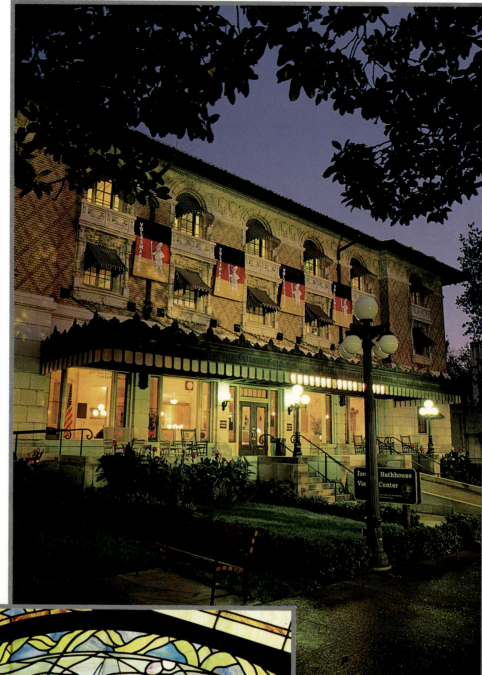

MATT BRADLEY PHOTOS

TOM TILL

Lake Conway

Sunflowers blossom among cyprus trees at Arkansas' first settlement.

Arkansas Post, the first community established in the state, was founded in 1686. Among the first women settlers was a group of "worthy but poor girls" who were sent as wives for men at the Post. Each woman's dowry was one cow and a calf, a rooster and five hens, a gun and ammunition, an ax, a hoe, and a supply of garden seed.

The Edwardian Inn in Helena, a bed and breakfast where the personal touch greets visitors.

MATT BRADLEY PHOTOS

From the book, *On a Slow Train Through Arkansaw*, a best seller on trains and in newsstands in the early 1900s:

"Maybe you have heard the story about the Arkansas native who said to a visitor that all we need in our state is a little more rain and a little better society. To which the visitor responded, 'That's all hell needs'."

TOM COKER

Above: Arkansas is second to none when it comes to American rice production.

Facing page: Wheat and wild-flowers—a natural combination.

MARK E. GIBSON

Sunrise over the Ouachita Mountains.

Above: Arkansas leads the nation in production of broilers.

Facing page: Winter in the Ozarks.

Arkansans are also cagey and shrewd business people. They tell the story of a chicken farmer who was peddling his wares one day in an open market in Fayetteville. He had sold every chicken from his large barrel except for one small, scrawny broiler in the very bottom. A farm woman came up and asked if he would show her what he had left. He picked up the old withered chicken and let her see it. She said she wanted to see another one. So he dipped down and shifted his arm around and then pulled up the same chicken and showed it to her from a different angle. "That's fine," she said. "I'll take both of them."

Above: Sailing rivals skiing on Lake Ouachita.
Right: Bull Shoals Lake—fun for avid fisher and water skier alike.

Arkansas in the latter part of the 19th century was famous for its lawlessness and its so-called "hanging judge," Isaac Charles Parker. Raiders on the western edge of the state included the Quantrill gang, Frank and Jesse James, Cole Younger, Belle Starr, and the Daltons. These colorful outlaws gave rise to the comment that "There is no Sunday west of St. Louis, and no God west of Ft. Smith."

Above: *Hangin' Judge Isaac Parker meted out justice in this courtroom in Fort Smith.*
Right: *The gallows outside Judge Parker's courtroom were a busy place.*

Facing page: *Arkansas is blessed with a wealth of trees.*

MATT BRADLEY

MARK E. GIBSON

Right: *The state capitol in Little Rock is the hub of Arkansas government and the closest replica to our nation's capitol in Washington, D.C.* **Above:** *The halls of the state capitol echo with pride.*

GENE AHRENS

Arkansas—a state connected by bridges and tradition. Seen here: Little Rock.

Right: *Arkansas boasts its own fine ballet troupe.*
Below: *Riverfront Park in downtown Little Rock hosts seasonal festivals.*

Facing page: *The Veterans Administration Hospital in Little Rock.*

MATT BRADLEY PHOTOS BOTH PAGES

Above: Riverboat rides are a treat on the Arkansas River.
Right: The Great River Road winds up and down the Delta.

Until 1970 the only means of crossing the Arkansas River near Conway was on the Toad Suck Ferry. The name came from a saloon located on the bank of the river. Locals would go to the saloon and suck on the bottles of moonshine until they were so bloated that the Indians said they looked like toads.

Left: *An afternoon at the Little Rock zoo—fun with furry friends.*
Below: *Restoration reigns supreme in Little Rock's Quapaw Quarter.*

Facing page: *The Old State House, Arkansas' first capitol, in downtown Little Rock.*

MATT BRADLEY PHOTOS BOTH PAGES

Above: *This old brick building was Arkansas' capitol in territorial days—long before statehood.*

MATT BRADLEY

Arkansas supports more than 300 species of trees. The largest tree is thought to be just outside Bentonville—an American sycamore that measures 21 feet in circumference and is 106 feet tall.

Right: *The Arkansas farmer—one of the nation's most productive.*
Below: *Farm machinery is a mainstay of Arkansas' livelihood.*

Facing page: *The work ethic still is embedded in the Arkansas mind.*

Arkansas has approximately 1,500 caves, most of them in the Ozarks. The best known is probably Blanchard Springs Caverns in Stone County, which is part of the Ozark National Forest. One column of calcite is more than 70 feet high, and the Cathedral Room is the length of three football fields.

Above: *Corncribs—a reminder of times past.*

Facing page: *The subterranean beauty of Blanchard Springs Caverns.*

Above: This sign, outside Gillett, could easily characterize any town in Arkansas. *Right:* The mill at War Eagle—home of Arkansas' largest crafts fair.

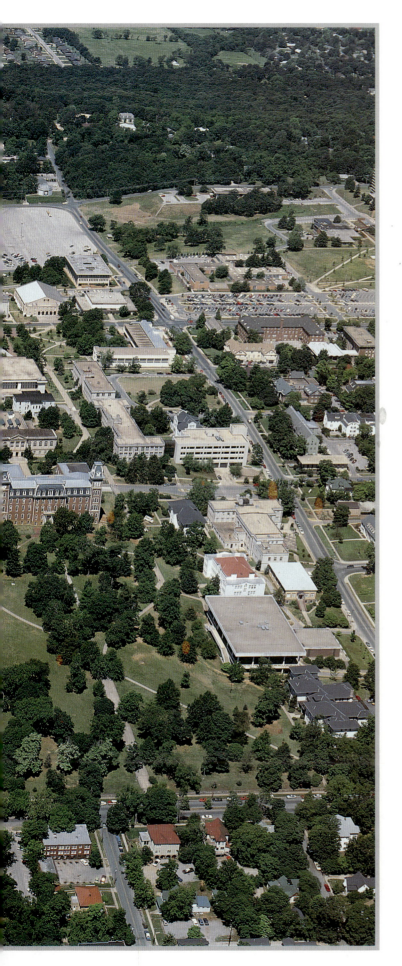

Probably the most celebrated small animal associated with the State of Arkansas is the razorback, the mascot of our University at Fayetteville. Legend has it that in about 1540, when Hernando de Soto crossed the Mississippi River into what is now Phillips County, his men brought with them 200 horses and a band of wild hogs, thus starting a long line of stock that has given Arkansas athletics a distinctive identity.

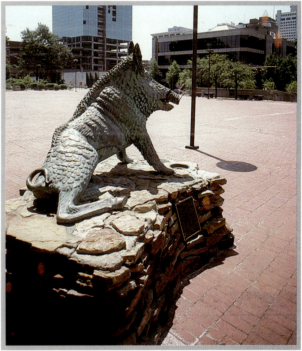

MATT BRADLEY

Left: The University of Arkansas, the state's largest educational institution, boasts state-of-the-art sports and athletic facilities.
Above: The Arkansas Razorback mascot is no stranger to the nation.

Left: *Whittling is part sport, part therapy.*
Below: *These Phillips-Chisholm wood carvings are representative of local handiworks.*

Facing page: *The seat of government for Washington County, Fayetteville.*

MATT BRADLEY PHOTOS

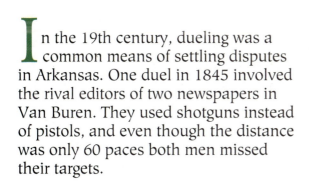

In the 19th century, dueling was a common means of settling disputes in Arkansas. One duel in 1845 involved the rival editors of two newspapers in Van Buren. They used shotguns instead of pistols, and even though the distance was only 60 paces both men missed their targets.

MATT BRADLEY

Right: Schools take a holiday and farm tractors cease activity when duck hunting season opens. *Below:* Hunters from all over the world converge on Stuttgart for the International Duck Calling Contest.

KEITH SUTTON

MATT BRADLEY

TOM COKER

Arkansans people are hard workers, or scrappers, as they're often called. They tell the story in North Arkansas about the chicken farmer who was driving his truck up a steep hill in the Ozarks. It was a brutal drive, and every once in a while he leaned out the truck window and banged the top of the cab with a big club. When he reached the crest of the hill he pulled over to the side and somebody came up to him and complimented him on the fine job of driving that brought that old truck up the hill. But why did he lean out and bang the top with that club? "Look," the farmer said, "I'm driving a two-ton truck, and I'm carrying four tons of chickens. And if I don't keep half of them flying, I'm in trouble."

Above: *A leading producer of soybeans, Arkansas agriculture is a pace-setter for the nation.*

Facing page: *In Little Rock, the courthouse of Pulaski County—the state's most populous.*

JIM LOW

Above: *It doesn't get any better than a bass fishing tournament on the Arkansas River.*
Right: *Arkansas fishermen get their training at a very early age.*

Facing page: *Many of the world's problems have been solved—daily—on the porches of Arkansas general stores.*

KEITH SUTTON

__Above:__ The Confederate cemetery in Helena.
__Right:__ Arkansas has it all when it comes to terrain.

From a funeral tribute in an Arkansas weekly newspaper in the late 1980s:

"With the exception of the two ladies, we use the term ladies in the loose possible sense of the word, who had the tasteless audacity to set in the entry way...at our mother's funeral and gossiped about family matters of which they know nothing, we wish to thank everyone who sent flowers, cards, food and attended mom's funeral out of true caring. Your sincere support during our time of sorrow was greatly appreciated.

'Life is not forever, I'll see you later. Leona'."

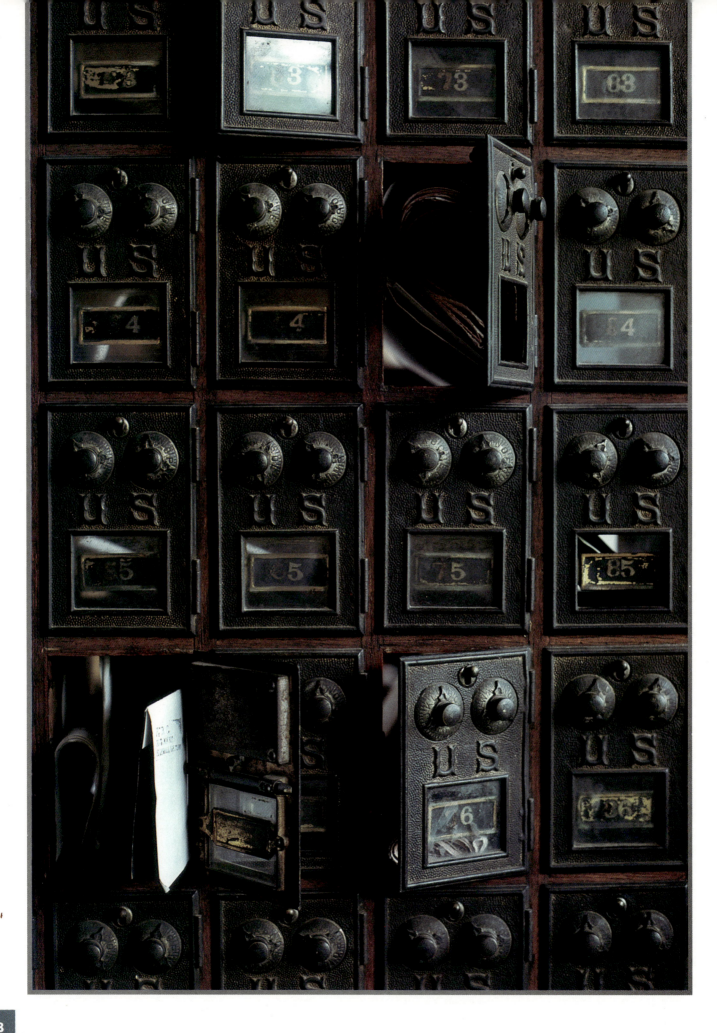

Above: If Hankins doesn't have it, you don't need it.

Facing page: The post office still is the federal government to many Arkansans.

Above: *A species native to Arkansas—the river otter.*
Left: *Autumn's paintbrush at Mulberry.*

In its history, Arkansas has lived under the rule of France, Spain and the newly founded United States. John Patterson, who was born in Arkansas in 1790 and lived here until 1886, summed up the stages of his life in this way:

> I was born in a Kingdom,
> Raised in an Empire;
> Attained manhood in a Territory;
> Am now a citizen of a State;
> And have never been one hundred miles from where I live.

MATT BRADLEY

Above: *A Saturday afternoon meeting of the minds.*

Facing page: *Down by the old mill house stream in North Little Rock.*

Above: The art of quilting is passed on to the younger generation at Mountain View.
Right: Pride in a stitch is readily evidenced in a homemade quilt.

Facing page: Pickin' and grinnin' at the Folk Festival in Mountain View.

MATT BRADLEY

The Buffalo is probably the best-known of the many small rivers in Arkansas, and certainly one of the most beautiful. It starts high up in Newton County, flows north, and then turns east to join the White River near Buffalo City. This is 150 miles away, when you factor in the winding nature of the river.

Above: *Wildlife—such as this unusual white opossum—has a chance in numerous reserves and refuges.* **Right:** *Reflections.*

TOM COKER

Left: Picking your own blueberries is half the fun of making the cobbler.
Below: Grandchildren can still shop at some of the places their grandparents did.

Facing page: The ones that didn't get away.

In 1830 Jim Bowie, living in Hempstead County, designed a knife for Stephen Austin of Texas. It was a long-bladed weapon that came to be called by most people the Bowie knife—but by others, the "Arkansas toothpick."

CHRISTIAN HEEB

Above: *The delights of an evening at Cajun's Wharf, on the banks of the Arkansas River in Little Rock.*
Right: *Highway 16 in Northwest Arkansas.*

Right: *Lakes and streams around Hot Springs interrupt horse trails.*
Below: *Water skiing on Greers Ferry Lake is some of the best.*

Facing page: *Campers enjoy the peacefulness and the natural beauty of Hot Springs National Park.*

Arkansas has the only known diamond field in North America. It is near Murfreesboro, Pike County, in the Ouachita Mountains. The Star of Arkansas, by far the largest diamond found in this field, weighed more than 15 carats.

Above: *Windmills harken to the past.*
Left: *This picturesque scene shows the open spaces of the "Natural State."*

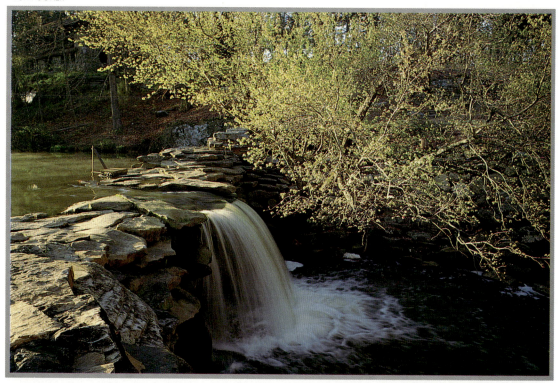

___

Above: *The country church—symbol of family and community in Arkansas.*

Facing page, top: *Petit Jean is one of a growing system of state parks.*
Bottom: *The Mt. Magazine overlook provides the pinnacle view of the state.*

Traffic on the Arkansas River grew in the 1850s. There were 317 steamboat dockings at Little Rock only from November 1858 through June 1859, an average of more than one per day. But by the beginning of the 20th century, railroads had taken over the transportation enterprise. In 1880 there were 822 miles of railroad; by 1890 this had grown to 2,200 miles. Progress shifted from river ports to railroad towns, which accounts for there having been two seats of government in a number of Arkansas counties.

MATT BRADLEY PHOTOS BOTH PAGES

Above: Murray Lock and Dam directs water through the heart of Arkansas.

Facing page: Farmers' markets give new meaning to the term "homegrown."

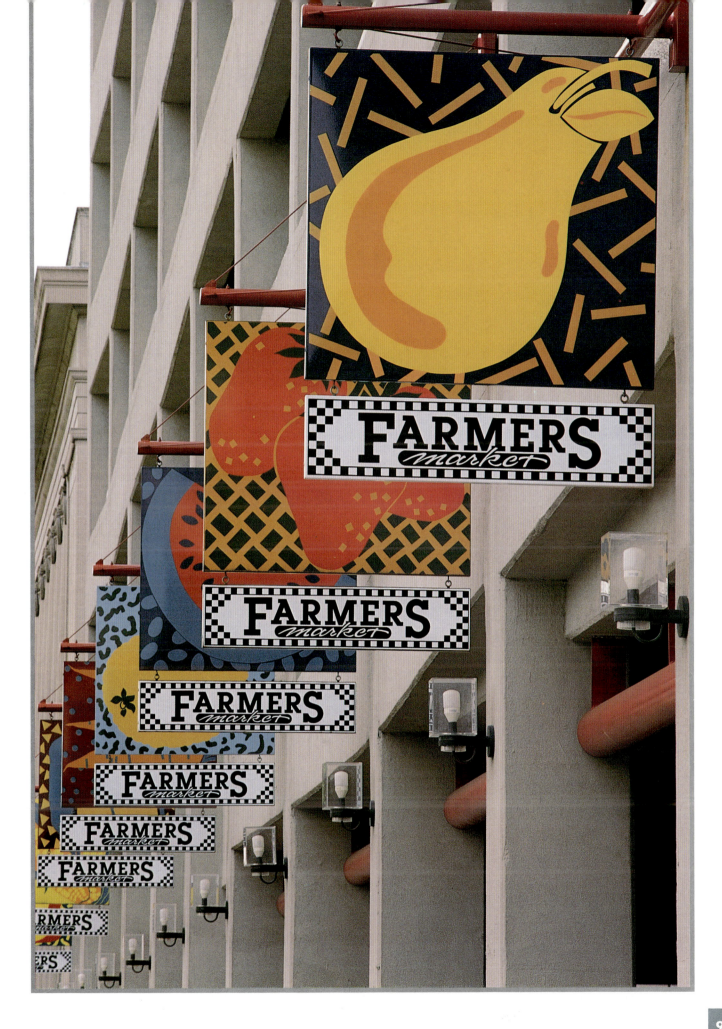

Above: *Beneath this spray of whitewater lies the mystical underworld of Blanchard Springs Caverns.*

Facing page, top: *One-room schools were the norm before electricity.*
Bottom: *Man and the land in harmony.*

From the advertising section of the *Arkansas Gazette,* June 28, 1825:

Wright Daniel's FERRY
Four Miles Below Little Rock

The subscriber respectfully informs Travelers and others, that he still continues his old FERRY, across the Arkansas River, four miles below the town of Little Rock, at the following rates:

For a large wagon and team	$1.00
Wagon with two horses	.75
Wagon or cart, with one horse	.50
Man and horse	.12$\frac{1}{2}$
Footman or loose horses	.06$\frac{1}{4}$
Each head of cattle	.06$\frac{1}{3}$
Hogs and sheep, per load	.50

Travelers can be supplied with corn, at 50 cents per bushel.

WILLIAM A. BAKE

Above: *Cattle graze peacefully on a pasture near Dover.*

Facing page: *An occasional general store like Bunche's in Kingston is a step back in time.*

Overleaf: *The majestic cliffs above the Buffalo River.*

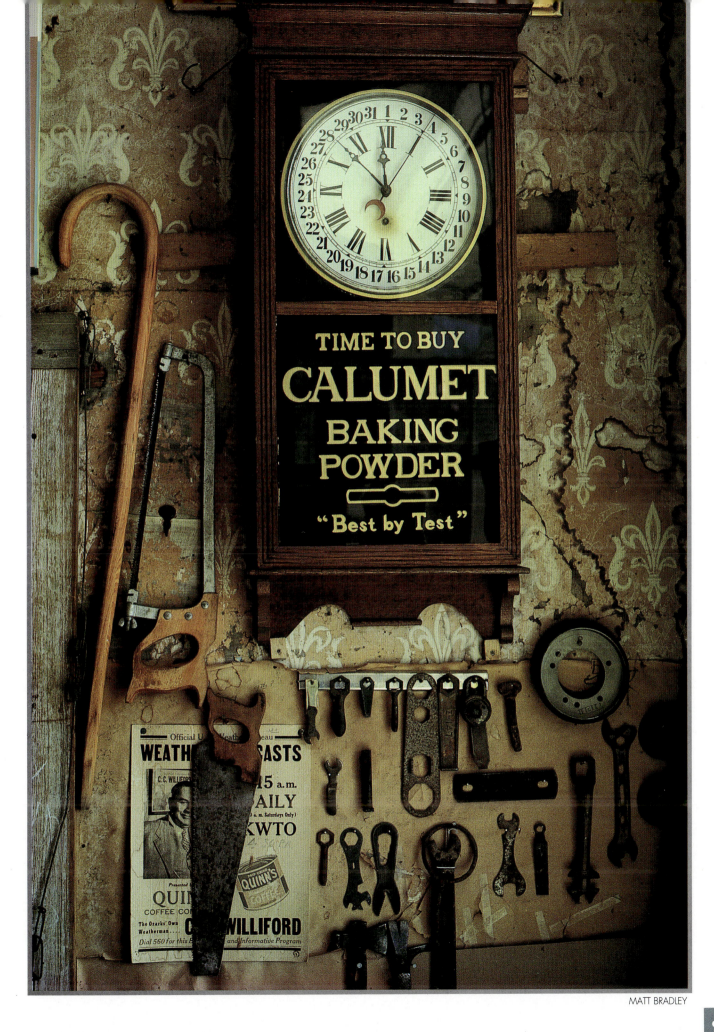

MATT BRADLEY